Reduction Fired

poems by
Jennifer Yeates Camara

Reduction *refers to the pottery method of firing a piece in low oxygen conditions – typically by slowly reducing the oxygen that feeds the kiln's fire. Some colours of glazes result from reduction that aren't achieved in oxidation.*

It may also be that the fuel-starved fire pulls oxygen from the clay itself, and in doing so draws elements from deep in the clay up to the glaze. This can make it harder to determine the precise outcome of the glazed piece.

Reduction can even change the texture of the clay.

This first edition published 2021 in Canada by Yeates Expressions

Copyright © Jennifer Yeates Camara

All rights reserved. This publication may not be reproduced, stored in a retrieval system, or transmitted, in any form or by any means electronic, mechanical, photocopying, recording or otherwise, without the prior permission of the author.

ISBN 978-1-7775728-2-2 (hardcover)
ISBN 978-1-7775728-1-5 (paperback)
ISBN 978-1-7775728-0-8 (EPUB)
ISBN 978-1-7775728-3-9 (MOBI)

Contact: yeatescamara.com

Front Cover, Back Cover and Insert photos©
by Jennifer Yeates Camara
Cover and Interior Design by Bright Wing Media

'Think simple' as my old master used to say – meaning reduce the whole of its parts into the simplest terms, getting back to first principles. – Frank Lloyd Wright

Gratitude

I am in awe at the support I have received over the years from so many.

With my deepest appreciation, I would like to thank certain people specifically who have encouraged my writing—my parents for their love of reading and the arts, my sisters (and friends) including Regan, Teresa and Alexandra, for their support of all kinds, my former employer Carmen, old friends like Dan Kirchner, Stacey Williams, Karen Zirk and Alex Watling, friends I've lost like Michelle and Marnie Cole, and the dear, dear friends I'm fortunate to have now.

Like many others, I also benefited from passionate teachers and librarians, and an extraordinary bookstore-owning couple, Brian and Ann Murdoch, all enthusiastic, knowledgeable people who shared their interests with me.

Contents

Winter — 1
- All's Quiet — 2
- Dynasty — 2
- Fire Towers — 3
- Estuaries — 4
- Rarely Seen — 4
- Friends, Family, Colleagues — 5
- Lovely — 5
- Scarecrow — 6
- Leaving — 7
- Alone after Nineveh — 8
- Flying — 9
- Place — 9
- Open sea — 10
- The Youngest — 11
- When I Needed It Most — 12
- Ugliness — 12
- Make the Best — 12
- Regrets — 14
- Late Autumn — 14
- The Leap — 16
- The Cliff — 16
- Pitt River 2016 — 18

Autumn — 21
- Chalk Drawings — 22
  - I. — 22
  - II. — 23
  - III. — 24

IV.	26
V.	26
VI.	27
VII.	28
VIII.	29
IX.	29
Confirmation	30
Thoughts After Reading Haiku	31
I.	31
II.	32
III.	32
IV.	32
V.	33
VI.	33
VII.	33
VIII.	34
IX.	34
X.	34
XI.	34
XII.	35
XIII.	35
XIV.	35
XV.	35
XVI.	36
XVII.	36
XVIII.	36
XIX.	36
XX.	36
XXI.	37
XXII.	37
XXIII.	37

XXIV.	37
XXV.	37
XXVI.	37
XXVII.	37
XXVIII.	38
XXIX.	38
XXX.	38
XXXI.	38
XXXII.	38
XXXIII.	38
XXXIV.	38
XXXV.	39
XXXVI.	39
XXXVII.	39
XXXVIII.	39
XXXIX.	39
XXXX.	39
XXXXI.	40
XXXXII.	40
XXXXIII.	40
XXXXIV.	40
XXXXV.	40
XXXXVI.	41
XXXVII.	41
XXXVIII.	41

Summer   43
    Enough   44
    The Hearth   46
    Passion   47
    Sighting   49

Dancers	50
New Moon	52
Medusa	53
Snowfall	57
Daydream	58
Warmth	58
Weather	60
Like the Wind	63
Exercise	64
"White Pine" - A.J. Casson	66
Homecoming	67
Cactus	69

Spring   73

Michelle	74
I.	74
II.	74
W.A.M.W.	75
I.	75
II.	75
III.	76
IV.	76
V.	76
VI.	77
VII.	77
VIII.	77
IX.	78
X.	78
XI.	78
XII.	79
XIII.	79

Winter

All's Quiet

rippling like the elephant's ear
or ticking tails like bulls
and cows, there is
no pattern or telling how
rare or often it bubbles
up and over the fenced
teeth and wide-brimmed lips,
and always when this
forked version spits out
I'm unprepared
to move as far
left or right as needed
to avoid it or
reconcile its appearance
with the teeth and lips
and face behind

Dynasty

Gentle and measured
   web-footed stepping of geese
   signaling beaks as tired wings rest,
Li Bai and Du Fu yet walk for me
   under the orchard's mottled shade
   with thoughtful nods and
   sage hands clasped behind

Fire Towers

Chilled trees
with branches empty
yet tipped in ready buds,
my fingers spread keen
watchmen for the hiding
scouts of summer
dressed in thicker fuller breezes,
making forays behind hills,
before its march
breaks onto the valleys
edging my palms,
so as not to be taken
by surprise
by its growing
mass crowding
out my cool
breath that my buds
crack and fall with
out opening
even

Estuaries

Eddies of them flow
past as bark mulch
in my palms hard and soft
pieces filling every sense
of cupped hands heel to nail
tips with all their types
of feeling I too easily forget
to look beneath the wood
dust to their soil and what's left
there that germinates
in me

Rarely Seen

No songs, it captivates
with silence of wings
that swim the airs
or fade when stilled
absent flits of dainty birds,
its nest away somewhere
a secure bough
the ideal perch protects
by vantage views,
nor colourful even
in beak or feathers,
but eyes compelling
as star giants ageing

their knowledge yet alive
to surrounding unknowns
and watchful even if
seeming indifferent
this owl heart

Friends, Family, Colleagues

Had just one feather pried
its hollow silk night line between
my soul and me, heart and bones,
that single keenly shanked
wound soon after quaking would start
to close then scar and I'd have stood
a good chance against you
Karasu[1] , not lain counting
the soft shafts to hurry on
this slowly blurring sleep

Lovely

An ocean of blue-white
  snow falls in pieces
  on faces jagged and peaked
  then fills in the lines
  of clear cuts and erosion
  with its luminous finery
  that flatters not hides them

---

[1] "Karasu is an ominous bird, different from a crow, raven, rook or blackbird", The Classic Tradition of Haiku - An Anthology, Edited by Bowers, Faubion; Dover Publications, Inc., 1996, note 1 page 14

And these ranges finally
   in winter are beautiful
   now bared of youth coloured
   flowers and green tree cover
   striking the eyes in air crisp
   or unseasonably warm as
   only mature women can
   stand angled with gashes
   and age shown or traceable
   and gaze leveled to meet
   one discerning as rare this
   honesty with awareness

Scarecrow

Every day
being dead I stand
a scarecrow
guard of the near empty
field, from these crows
perched all atop me
each gripping tight
to lean one claw up
to its beak and eat what
grain was left,
as I yet turn my
in and out pain
ful grimace to one
to chase them
all away

Leaving

It became comfortable
the imprints of the many
uneven stones gnarled roots
and matted leaves etched
the length of me through
my own weight all released
until it became un
comfortable without their
rough engraving and pressure
too familiar and too old
to trace the memory, so
I now find this stance
on my own weight held up
through the soles of me
and this skin smoothed
like petals basking though un
mapped and untouched but
by the bees and humming
birds buzzing and hovering
respectfully or fingertips caressing
gently, all so unexpectedly
intriguing that unnerved with
anticipation I'm yet startled
by how much it feels even
innate deep-rooted through
and through me being me
unbranded it's become glorious

Alone after Nineveh

Sincerely I miss it
but not its shade
or shelter from
the all exhausting dryness
of the sweltering winds
and parched air
surrounding to the
point of swooning,
truthfully I do
miss my bottle-gourd
plant I didn't seed or grow
its unexpected yet
not the least unsettling
presence being such calm
company I took its sudden
withering too deeply when
I must have known I wouldn't
take it when it came
time to go

Flying

Flying arches in the great wide blue,
A heart peaceful and lively
Like a child running arms full span,
Wanting others to come to feel this,
They look up, sadly, mouthing 'loner'

Place

If in the sea I lived
below the surface
there the endless
overhead stretching
of waves with their ripples
would take my heart
in calm and smooth steppes
following them, and not
bracing for constant assaults
to my soul tide after tide
marching past all my rocks
endlessly on this coast
where I live

Open sea

Pronged leaves
of the Japanese
Maple buoy slightly
in the rainy air, their points
curved down to keep
the bodies up
from its streams while
clutching each a drop
for added strength, so
what appeared as
stoic honour all along
was fragile fear
of one leaf in a sea
of others holding nothing
anchored or substantial
in the ceaseless
currents it rides
only and never sails

The Youngest

When I've finished stooping
      picking up the toys
      of those older and cleared
      and packed away their boards
      of strategy and posturing
      they only abandon when they can
      play outside in life
When I've set out ideals
      by words imperfect and divine
      and aimed to show them
      in laboured example falling
      short and getting up again
      to have them take all in and keep none
Then I sit cupping the hot tea
      and drifting each iris to the distant
      Montana clouds unbound
      long-necked California sequoia
      Alberta plains spread to no horizon
      and Pacific waves breaking until
      broken only by the crickets
      of my twilight as the fireflies
      float outside my darkening pane
      blinking neon signs to remind me
      another sleepless night is near

When I Needed It Most

A dear one's
false defense testified
as truth lays
open the heart to salt
water's unfeeling cold,
and vulture box jellies'
long-tailed tentacles,
so finally
when all stinging
slows the flesh
is dead or so
I hope

Ugliness

Afterward
having taken my only
pumpkin skinning the insides
for garbage and making
target practice of its shell
they say that wasn't really
fun like they expected

Make the Best

Are you sure I am
in fact an orphan haven't
I from time
to time groves even

forests of older wiser
siblings plus saplings
looking up to
me and clouds of aunts
writing gentle cards in tight
or round calligraphy looking
down fondly from
a distance and here
on the coast my seas
of cousins I see
often outside and when
they're playing in the
wind they always wave in
deed and every day
grandpa sun isn't away
working he glows full of
stories or steals a smile at
me from behind his
white papers now and then as
if not to let grandma see him
be less than full
grown and each night her moon
face serene is sweet as a
lullaby that impels me to
smile sweetly too so yes in fact
with all these in sight
daily I can't be
an orphan can I?

Regrets

Time passes in families
like it doesn't all inclined
for ease or vain in false
discernment returning
to cache our secrets where stored
before despite breaches withstood
by one and all over
time and trued up sense
with calm eyes reminding us
in times of approaching
war or great attainment
those who watched us
grow may make our
worst consiglieres

Late Autumn

I visit daily at least
not from piety though
that house draws me
or I should say
its shingles sliced so
thin but scaled tight
enough to keep out
tree-bending snows deep
trolling winds or loads
of bricked rain
needling down about
that couple by a

fire inside, as
incredibly those
shingles fence
in warmth as cool
as it gets on
their other side, and the
couple don't know how
tight the fence posts
grip the soil against
the trawling storms
or how the coals' heat
stays around them
how I look weathered
and worn at those brickstrong
shingles in
awe confused at
their impossibility

The Leap

Many charmed by truth
   they say are not enough
   beguiled to stand firm
   for it like you once
   felt drawn by me to look
   close with your all
   but ambition and
Just as many are wanting
   out of what's missing
   to confirm that charm
   of a breeze as constant
   affection that my heart
   leapt the chasm with all
   sincerity outstretched and
   fell and fell and fell

The Cliff

So eager to grow
to try again to learn
to listen to your elders
to proper authority
to even we fragile ones
so easy to droop our blooms
or shake in bleak or
raw weather then
perk upward after
you invested emotionally
and before your assistance

was complete
of course I fell and
farther daily and no
I'm not the least sorry
even if you are even if
integrity has attached
its chord from you
to a soul other than
this one that looks toward
your face like it were fixed
just to reflect the moon
light closer so I won't
anymore be in the dark
afraid and that
chord forever
divided the soul
from its face even then
I couldn't regret the fall
or every day descent
to this place
for look – on this slope
the flowers here I've
never seen before

Pitt River 2016

I remember
clearly as the shallow river
itself being carried
along by my hands barely
stepping through the stoney
bed and body
stretched out
behind them coasting its
surface down waters
deepening to the neck standing
to finally swim awhile before
climbing out and up bank
and sailing yet again for
how I've loved always the
water until until the earth
and you whispered
to offer friend
ship even everlasting
and I surrendered
all future rights to
liquid suspension for legs
of needles to walk
to you and be
close that I might for
once know
the warm rays of that
foreign ship indeed
and suffered those pins
gladly though it

was never anchored
but drifting along
toward its own
other mooring so there
were no more legs or
rivers for me but Ariel's
dry tears and others' dreams
losing child-like wonder
and a woman's heart at
once

Autumn

Chalk Drawings

I.

It lays with me
full against my back
rested on my shoulder cuff
roped around my waist
your voice
a weight
familiar as childhood
friends so
compelling strangely
warm and clear
at once

a ladle it skims
my heart
beats and cups them
there noodles hung limply
from the lip

almost tender if
I could bear
its tenderness not
being
for me

it only lays beside
a moment that
sound
your voice
a pause

that breaks against
these walls of my
empty room
an echo only
for me

so soft like
evening
and welcome so
it aches
when it moves
on

II.

My deepest organs
now knead them
selves thin
to think I was
close enough
to touch your
face
arm
back but
held back enough
to map
your downward gaze
in thought-out speech the
strong rounded strides
of your walk
your sideways
turns and relaxed
hands but not

their end not
their heading
away

so sung I
was by each tree
branch and leaf
to see the
forest ran
off somehow just
when I hard-clenched all
my scarred intestines
smiling bravely and

stepped in

III.

(after the modern ballet)

Pulling apart each fibre
of muscle every cell
reaching up fingertips heels
seeking breezes twisting shoulders
this way then
that while stretching
out to new air yet experienced
places moments some hung
some hyper feelings to be
felt deep in the blue black
waters past the drop off
too thick to search
with eyes I
exalt in this

driven exploring wide this heart
mind and not shallow
sight like the others
not with eyes
only two or
thousands hungry
as if starving like rats
well fed and never satisfied
my craving is for
growth refinement even
boiling off the dross expanding
up and out with no
regret for shedding
scales or muscles
overstretched to
aching from
the beauty of it all
but only that I may

have so soon out
grown you
may have

all along been
past your
reach

IV.

You still don't know
   me off the gossip pages
neither the explorer nor
   the scientist I am
you rarely asked
   questions never good ones
only listened, yes sweetly
   combed your careful replies
   I guess to taste them, play
the great jazz music
   -ian sounding off another
answer to each call
   when getting sounds
   gifted and boxed large
took out the notes
   to respond in kind and
   never heard the music

V.

My oceans still lap
   the dry sand away
      asking why
         did you why
      did you not
know the waves go on
whether your soles weight
the sepia ash
or step through its dust

My oceans wash still
   the wet sand ahead

    climbing up
        to fall back
    to inch up
waves the tide spurs on
your face shining there
or on a cloying lake

My oceans stop not
   for any sand or man
      who swims pooled water
   still when he'd have sailed
for boundless seas

VI.

And yet and yet
despite cat-like stepping
through your widespread ferns
noble and striking
like stinging nettle
before I pressed forward
admittedly I know
little maybe nothing of this
place we lingered changing
in meaning as in aspect
where viewpoints draw
back curtains on new insights
and further greens that colour
the scenes thus revealed
along with those long struck
admittedly I know
my stealth and stirring
only and not who you saw

brush past your fronds
and yet and yet
before leaping on
I pause in interlude
surprised to find I feel
this sorry for you

VII.

These sweltry days
that drape the stems and boughs
thick with overripe flowers
even while steaming
all skin disclosed
they make
the mind like muscle
limber and bending
to be revised
as sweat and moisture
ease the mold of clay
Yes, sculling through
these hours readily
incites unhinging
and connecting thoughts
to new ones where the old
melt from the torrid
weight of summer cloud
to bead the surface
of belief
So while my head bows
restful and content
to note your progress
of departure,

my lashes less ponderous
may yet skip about
the compass catching
one or two more
recent edits to your
habits, face or hair
before all beads of
you have all
but burned away

VIII.

Indeed some prefer nettle,
some daisy and bulrush,
while snapdragons and lupines
crane their fine-spun necks
not toward them, but up up to
sun and moon and mountain peak

IX.

A cormorant drops into
   my thinking slick and near
   soundless but for a small splash
   from black mercury dropping
   quickly uncorking head then body
   flashing a round eye that smiles
You slink in and out my thoughts
   with little fuss or splash but calm
   settles like an eye content the storm
   threatened no longer comes or
   might as well for all it matters

Confirmation

Perhaps I

was just tied
to your image as
I made it since
we met, to
each virtue I imputed
from you, your
manner deeds and
seeming interest in
me that I

waited
hopefully for your
answers spread
simply before
me telling why

you waved me over
times over or
met me when
I sat down just to say
you didn't, why even I
stretched my
tips toward
you hoping no one'd
notice enough to guess
it just to hear you
say so gently you
never noticed it, really

any answer wanting
to return
those virtues to where
I'd put them wanting
not to accept they weren't
there or those or that
perhaps I

was so looking for
those answers
of yours just to not see
that it didn't
matter indeed
if they all were
there when you
didn't want to be

Thoughts After Reading Haiku

I.

Karasu[1] faces
off two crows –
maybe a third[2] – who
will survive will
I, these
thoughts of mine?

---
1   See footnote 1 under earlier poem, "Friends, Family, Colleagues"
2   In English, three crows together are called a murder of crows.

II.

Skeletal
clouds float clear
waters together
calmly without
flesh neither
judged nor
judging

III.

Weekend shoes
in the train
standing so
differently from
in the week...how
can one know
which is true?

IV.

In summer
evening sun
tree shadows
lay napping
on soft
green grass

V.

A crowd of
June mountains
pose all dressed
in dark-green
gowns so fine they
don't dare move

VI.

Hear the
café tables –
each lively
in its own
tongue, nested
birds in the city

VII.

Man's unrhythmic
summer cicadas
of road repair bridge
work and bus tours
neither drown nor dull the
plush regal trees warm
conversations and
flowing smiles around
them all natural

VIII.

Tree branch
shadows spread
dark latticed vines
beyond the lawn
toward my sunny
courtyard seat

IX.

Steamed blossom
perfumes – a
thick warm stew
not sweet yet
soothing still

X.

In the distance
lines of wild silver
horses gallop
forward – shining
currents in the Strait

XI.

Hototogisu[1]
your mourning time but half-spent
my duties won't keep

---

[1] "translated as cuckoo, wood thrush....It...migrates to Japan in May and stays until autumn...The song is a strong but mournful cry...Hototogisu is also known as the ... 'bird of disappointed love'", The Classic Tradition of Haiku -An Anthology, Edited by Bowers, Faubion; Dover Publications, Inc., 1996, note 2 page 9

XII.

Wind currents
dance pines in
dramatic
slow ballets,
maples in
lively jazz

XIII.

With gasps and coughs,
near-drowning, a
Father's rescue
revives even
my child-weak heart

XIV.

My right wing
grabbed – sharp you
came for me! –
snatched from the
hard earth's eyes
your Eaglet

XV.

Deceptively
complex my
eyes speak but
simple truths
why wonder?

XVI.

Clear creek water
in city streets – oh
for a heart sincere!

XVII.

Wind and rain, moving
plain and forthright,
transfigure leaving
no tattoo or scar

XVIII.

Sometimes I'm
Kirikou and
some Karaba –
where child or
thorn remains

XIX.

Safely moored boat
ropes creek against subtle
wakes of smaller ships
speeding by at a distance

XX.

Your brown eyes swept
away in the currents
of my blues, you would
not brave the water!

XXI.

No match for peregrine's speed or
sight, some yet reign with soft speech
and a firm gloved hand, held out

XXII.

An obscured fond moon
brushes starry fingers through
strands of sun-lit sea

XXIII.

Waiting for winter
in August it seems better
to know than not know

XXIV.

They gnaw on, smiling
my meal's coming – a surprise!
in pangs I 'wait crumbs

XXV.

Trapped within clear walls
I pound hoping while they muse
'What a funny dance?'

XXVI.

Joseph freed for dreams
Who realized his clean hands?
Who saw a rapist?

XXVII.

Lands echo. I'll not see
Guangdong again but at sea
the Pearl River runs on

XXVIII.

Me too, if layered
in pine bark, needles and combs
would feel my sap's safe!

XXIX.

A steady brush of
sweeping wind strokes erodes,
not rare hacking storms

XXX.

Kindness dealt cruelly
the stooped pack jabbers, scheming
to lick the mud off

XXXI.

Tied a float in seas
of ceaseless helpful chatter
I pray to be freed

XXXII.

Eyes slowly unsheathed
sharper than the dawn beside
and warm straight away

XXXIII.

Sinking in soft waves
yet held afloat by them, I
guess, my hand in yours

XXXIV.

Ancient sailors raised
eyes up to read sure stars, not
man-made lights or signs

XXXV.

His soul misplaced, the
bassist holds his empty case
puzzled – what comes next?

XXXVI.

The tree's roots pulled up –
all their knots and earth exposed –
its leaves fall, to clothe.

XXXVII.

Her cutting words lunged
at the meek seller, his boy
casts at hers pity

XXXVIII.

The sea ran in – I
thought it mine and laughed! It drew
off…O how I sighed!

XXXIX.

My soul chose him whose
acts were tender – but not mine
still, buds coax a smile

XXXX.

I invited you
in but unsure you stood there
What's a host to do?

XXXXI.

Old maids smirk, elbow
me and nod at the lone man
walking by aloof

XXXXII.

I felt more for him
than you have ever felt – you
think I regret it?

XXXXIII.

Room 101 was
cruelest after – I never
felt for friends the same

XXXXIV.

You saw more rows of
petals than most...so you know
the chrysanthemum?

XXXXV.

(no renga – answering verse)

It's only in daylight
I can forget your face – each
night's moon reminds me!

Soon hototogisu[1] leaves...
the real moon will reappear!

---

1   See footnote 1 for earlier poem, "Thoughts After Reading Haiku – XI"

XXXXVI.

Canopies of leafed
branches so beguiling they're
welcomed sun or shade

XXXVII.

(no renga – answering verse)

How many million
cherry blossom buds in snow
entombed wait to rise?

A spring dawn must soon break – then
casting off white sheets will pink petals unfurl

XXXVIII.

This bark of northern trees withstands years
of elements even taking in fire to bend
into a box or good canoe bearing people
and their many needs – yet oh how a host
of bugs though weaker burrow on and on and on

Summer

Enough

I fan out my
bare boughs like
veins pushing into
the sky's flesh as
though trying to
draw out enough
blood to live and
even bear
the fruit I'm
sure I harbour
seeds of
somewhere
inside. I've seen
other trees as
if convinced the
pink ruffles of the
cherry's blossoms and
rustling leaves of the
ever-green are
mocking me
for all they
don't see.
      But just
then the same
spirit that tosses them
in showy display
moves me too, and while
my limbs swaying
in the empty

heights may entice
no sweet
swallows, the grand
flocks and royal
eagles alight
to me to stand
on branches strong
enough to bear
their weight,
tall enough to
reach their path
of sky, and though
unseen by others my
roots stretch for
miles like veins into
the earth's flesh
drawing enough
water to outgrow
the rest and
one day
dress each bough
of mine in great, broad
leaves that will
shade groves
of other,
smaller trees from
the sun they
cannot bear.

The Hearth

Returning cool gusts
having chased off
youthful summer currents,
the crisp air in
increasing aloofness
crisps in turn the leaves
it rushes, closing windows
and doors and we turn
up the heat
inside

Autumn matures
us all
all that is natural
even love like mine
for you   so al-
though past thoughts of
sweet romance played
my mouth and limbs to
free-running laughter, now
they are gathered down
in stillness and brewed
to ferment such that
my passion's rising
scent would surely
intoxicate, were you
only near enough to
its perfume, compelled
to taste its fullness

surround your heart and feel
its soul-satisfying warmth
in your throat   until
inebriated past
consciousness, passed
out from its effects, so deep
you'd sleep!   and then –
on waking body
spent, tongue coated and
head fogged in by
real love's change
to your temperature
your rousing
thought incites
your reaching out for
yet another
drink even as
your eyes ask mine
for a chaser

Passion

Even the wind
in passionate storm
does not
press
the skin
with force it
knows, intensity
should be
surrounding

requiring
resistance
just to hold
one's ground, that
power
and strength
are not
profound and
pressure
only draws
reaction once
lifted

For the heart
of true courage
is in one's
chest, a
look, the
setting of the jaw
and lips
and not
in fingertips

Sighting

Like the first pulse of an earthquake
under deep waters I sent forth my hunger
for you wide as the seas believing
both that we were meant to be and to be
with you now too real so as if hidden
under deep waters, I send forth my hunger
(for you)

Atop a towering lighthouse surrounded
by foam the beacon of my mind burns bright
through thick fog it wears thin as a cape while
warning the ship I seek from my shores yet
welcoming it too to my safe harbour covered
by foam and the beckoning of my mind that burns bright
(through thick fog)

Calling your name to the unpopulated
canyon I found the sound of it answered back
to me unsettling as the first pulse of an earthquake
caught on sonar or a lighthouse beacon startled
by a ship's touch on its shrouded cape, for in my heart's
canyon I find the sound of your name answering back
(to me)!

Dancers

Seduced
by distractions the
quick movements of
shallow waters and
the thinnest veils, your
eyes grow tired
blurred from
fast smiles and frequently
arched
brows taken
in then mistook
by them

While down
in the thick
forest, I'm left
waiting for you to
look through
dancing leaves to
see honestly
how the subtle pools of
my eyes run deep, an
endless supply of
dew trickling down
chestnut roots
coating the quiet
yet vibrant
Georgia O'Keefe flowers
I grow for you

leaf to pink blossom
and the petals of
my lips pause
in mute anxiety to
be pressed to your
most open pages

Perhaps, you
should visit
Arabia's moving
sculptures of sands
a land
where reserve
and furore meet,
ask the Sheiks
for salve they
know – the best
dancers are revealed
in the potent silence
of their fingers, not
the earthquakes
of their hips

New Moon

new moon at perigee
my force
imperceptible
to you is
no less grave
my winter-white glow
buoyed still in a cool
indigo sea
admired only by
you unmindfully
in passing remains
a piercing beacon
unmanned at present
though routinely taken
note of

when sun's golden lid
lowers tired of light
summer's playful
affection you took
for true
love its full moon
reduced to a sliver and

cashmere breezes feel
unforgivably cold
look up I'll not
have changed
clear and bright I
love you though
it burns
not

Medusa

they keep coming
to me

Medusa

every look in my
direction
carefully made
indirect pursued
valiantly
but only to be
destroyed...I
wonder -
was Medusa
ugly
as
they say
or just
saw herself
that way,
reflected in

steel blades of
touch without
warmth that
struck with
the sharpness of
an ever hungry
need, all the while unwanted
held
too close to be
comforted then
let
go
at the first sign
of dusk for more
intriguing
pursuits like
drinks with friends
and talk of the next
battle for
sport

i grew
snakes for
hair to hold
the venom
secreted
from this
heart loaded
too heavily
with all
they hate
about themselves and if

they hiss
it's only because
like any monster I've
long since
lost
my own
right
to scream

but they
keep coming, pickscaling
me until
they crest
the height of
what they once
thought
a mountain
worth climbing
only to see yet higher
mountains and
foes more
legendary
than I to
vanquish but

there
is where they are
undone
not
by the monsters of
their own
reflection but

those who wear
beauty
as a mask
to hide
monstrosities
within

and while we
Medusas
may not win
against our
warriors we survive
long enough to
see them fall
in the arms
of a lady
by a lake
who dances
tree boughs down
around them stroking
them to sleep for
a thousand years

Snowfall

watching
sifted out flakes
of snow drift
downward past
naked branches in
writhing anguish frozen
mid-posture as
long ago things
I wonder
could your touch
be as soft, effortless
land so light
on my skin my eyes
run after each
sweet tingling to
find it already
disappeared
make past tense
all my grief
nakedly exposed to you
statues in permafrost
frozen forms that
feel no more
nor cause
me pain?

Daydream

For all the sharpness of my mind,
the vivid pictures it creates
and each imagined sense, I find
my wants unfilled, my heart not sated
from its ache to taste and feel
your mouth, your skin, and though I wait
as if expecting soon to share
the world with you that I create
with this imagined love, I find
my bones yet longing for your weight,
for all the sharpness of my mind.

Warmth

I only
realized
today
what it was and
how it started this
always wanting
more

this standing
shivering and
vulnerable
palms outstretched
to the crackling logs
of your days glad
at each spark

of time knowing
only the need
to get
warm

recalled being buried
so deep
in blankets and
all the
coats
mom could find that
come morning
I would dress
under covers
and hurry down
to sit inside
the window
box of sun-warmed carpet
with both hands holding
my cup

I'm still
rummaging
for comforters for
smiles and
approving looks and
time with you
to lie beneath to
place between me and
the cold

so even now
there are times

flakes blow through
the cracks
and frost maps out
my window pane
and all the flames
and coats
and sun
are not enough and
I just
wanted you
to know
I realized
today
it wasn't you that I'll
always be wanting
more
warmth

Weather

Not a fantasy
of you
goes by
without
your smile

the rest may
change with
time and
weather or how
I feel, but

mostly
the weather

morning sunshine looks
to like while rainsoaked
lanes and
tarnished
clouds are full
of compliments
and holding
hands

afternoon sun
burns
anticipation
on my skin

evening's
all undressed
a fresh cool
tongue and
hands that move
subtly with
the breeze
until
moisture in
the air clots
thick and the
grass tips
wet

come
what may

out
of doors,
each hope
and fancy is
inclined in
mood and
movement
really by
each smile
from you,
warm in any
clime and ripe
with I've
got you, don't
worry so
I don't
when you
smile my
love, you
really should
smile

more often

Like the Wind

Like the wind
you rush through
my hair and lift
the edges of my clothes

or float by
with a passing caress,
like the wind,
caring not what or
whom
you move
or touch, such
that they stop
to readjust
or turn and bend
their head to brace
for impact, seeking shelter
in a raised shoulder

Like the wind
remarking not
the mark you leave
on quiet hearts
ruffled by
the beauty of you
brushing by
while your eye
is ever fixed ahead
of them and their hearts
follow a ways

unable to name
the feeling that caught them
for a time except
to know
we cannot love
that which can't
be still

like the wind

or ambitious men
with eyes too full
of horizons
to gather the earth
is round

Exercise

Spent
so long measuring
with only logic
all blade
unyielding focus
to exhaustion
concentrated anguish
sweating from
my pores as
blood

Had to learn
instead to
flex
each muscle shred

of my feeling
heart
pumping the iron
will through the
walls of wants
of which
I've no control
until my
empathy is strong
enough to love even
me
even now –
to accept what flows
presently
throughout this body
works blue-collar hard
to keep me
fed today and fighting
illnesses I'll not be
taken with
to name –
to understand
this day is better
than tomorrow for
it's the only
measure of the past
from where
I've come

"White Pine" – A.J. Casson

Here, nothing is as it seems
crisp, stark and sculptured
leans a windblown tree

The lifeless rocks are painted
clustered spots on muted tones
their bulky forms resemble seals
basking in a coming storm

Even the white clouds
are blown contrary to the wind

Moving away from your breath
a flimsy clay form

I await destruction indifferent
your slender shape becomes a strain
my blemished soul against your brown shroud
like colour splats on stone graves

Reaching for the tree of life
I search the naked structure
nothing, it seems, is there

Homecoming

when,
when will I
read the Braille of
your lips with
the tips of
my own
lay the hollow of my
cheek to rest on
your cheek bone
untangle your strands
from my hair
with fingers made
it seems
for the task
and sweep their thickness
back to let the light
of your face shine
full on mine
as my eyes
unwrap each gift
of words expressed
in looks
tied thoughtfully
with thick,
curved ribbons
of brow   when
will I be dressed
in your arms
and chest with

your palms so
peacefully at rest,
on shoulder blades or
breasts, supplying
all the support
I'll ever need
when   will I
at last enjoy
the glassshattering
touch of that
most pursued
caress, a
smile that
says I love
you now, I
love
you just

as you
are

Cactus

A soothing aloe
or milk-swelled cactus
in mid desert
I grow
inconspicuously rooted
waiting
for your need of

healing
balm to cover
wounds sustained
from the sharptongued
animals

liquor that
actually quenches
those thirsts
of yours
and restores lifefluids
seared off by
the unobstructed
fervour
of success

Some profess
to prefer the
beauty of
tropical blooms –
blind to their brief
flowering as they are

many and quickly
replaced

but oh love look
and see –

I grow green
where all else
is brown I
will nourish, sustain
and satisfy
not only
your eyes and
cactus blossoms are
even more
lovely being
unexpected
and from
no obvious
water source

Spring

Michelle

(who lost her battle with bi-polar depression Feb 8, 1995)

I.

I watched her drown; my hand I never brought
within her reach. I could not see the foe
she fought, the swirl and dragging of the flow
that often bound her struggling limbs and caught
her heart. The eyes I knew were always fraught
with tiring battle ever on the throws
of being lost; I thought it would be so
always. The more she weakened, more I sought
to cheer her from the shore.
                        Upon the sand
of this dry life I look where she should be.
Around me spreads a bare and graven land;
the woods, now huddled sticks of leafless trees,
and all the world looks dead from where I stand.
I wonder if she thought the same of me.

II.

They tell me that you feel no more the pain
That often traced your mouth when sweet you smiled.
Your laughing eyes e'er wet with some new trial
Are dry, and all that falls to earth is rain.
Yes, even washed away is that old stain
Of sin; the wages paid, you left the vile
And hurtful world behind, and Satan's guile
Will never wound your loving heart again.
But while these benefits I do admit
I also know that in your darkened sleep

Your eyes no more enjoy the ocean lit
With sun or moon, nor morning mists that creep
Past sleeping trees, nor bird, nor bee. For things
You'll miss, though painlessly you rest, I weep.

W.A.M.W.

I.

What almost moves within
prudence fully armoured cannot contain
it cannot lay hold of it to know it

Without a moment wasted
twice a thought begins the pattern
how difficult then to alter it!

When attitude mothers words
too ripe to cling to cautious branches
the expecting ear will hear them thud.

II.

Glances, like pebbles, fall into my soul
   sending rings to the bank of my knowledge
Each slow movement passes through me
   like water through my fingers
   and leaves my mind so crisp, so fresh
That soft smile like gentle rain,
   like the gentle rain that loosens an avalanche
   yes, even an avalanche of joy.
His smile, surfacing from his suffering
   like light from the dimmed east,
     to warm the body and even the heart.

III.

He is innocent
        mourning imperfection
He is loving-kind
        Articulating comfort to a depressed ear
His spirit is reclusive
        brooding beneath his magma, plates and crust
His feelings are a fathomless sea
        coveting wreckages in shadowy combs
He is faithful
        enduring the tightening bonds of each coming day.

IV.

Sing to his heart, my soul
find voice and sing to his heart with joyfulness
sing to his heart with rejoicing in your eyes

Agitate yourselves, o limbs!
agitate yourselves and dance
agitate yourselves in dances of jocund mirth.

Tremble because of him; yes
tremble with shiverings –
tremble and shiver at the wonder of him.

V.

Enliven my senses with substantial sayings
   taste my mind with full-bodied words,
      my thoughts with flavourful phonemes;
Utter syllabic echoes through consonant caves –
   for your speech is delicious,
      concretely satisfying with abstract nourishment.

VI.

Steadily inconstant feelings
    stem the refreshing shade of his stable thoughts
        while old roots suffer to support that quivering trunk,
        slowly drawing sustenance in aged weakness
    yet, his balanced mind precludes his fall
as he awaits the passing of ephemeral emotions.

VII.

His eyes perceive the very pathways of my breath,
    and even my sighs he seems to understand.
Is he not one of the sons of men?
    surely, he is also made of clay
    thrown from the same divine hand as I;
But a vessel full of understanding and insight he is,
    brimming with knowledge and truth.

VIII.

I listen until my bones proceed to ache
    but my unweaned lips babble unintelligently
I observe his heart fasting in grief;
    yet each naïve response heaps ashes upon his head.
Seeing my master's spirit restless,
    I attempt to amuse him with immature frivolity
Inexperience floods my streams of tender expressions
    drowning that one it seeks to refresh.

IX.

Like the mist of early morning
   wisps of you cling to my thoughts
Like the rhythmic waves
   your memory laps my soul endlessly
Like spring poplar leaves
   my eyes shimmer once blown by the sight of you
As flowers excite in meadow breezes,
   my spirit stirs when you walk by me.

X.

Your hands play
   concertos on ivory veins
     while Chopin conducts my force

Your fingers strike
   chords of threefold thought
     with cultured skill

Your eyes read
   my spiritual bars
     and render them as music

XI.

Who knows what evil lurks therein?
   those in pursuit of it chase the air
     it swims through the desperate swells
     and traverses the mad shore;
   the posses of wisdom and caution lag
while my love skulks in the shadows of your heart.

XII.

My master's crown is splendid:
        his grey-headedness is heavy in glory
His endurance is mighty;
        the sun's armies pale his skin, but he withstands them.

He comforts with summer's breeziness
        sighs and pauses diffuse his warmth.
He cannot conceal his regal gait –
        ponderously, he steps with majestic slowness.
His name means protector;
        wielding insight, he guards the spirit of his fellow.

XIII.

I see him always
   I see him always above me
      How is depth will be always above me

His righteousness is far-reaching
   His righteousness outreaches me
      His righteousness outreaches my grasp

He is sadness
   He is sadness, swelling
      He is sadness swelling up to devour

-As twigs will dam a swollen stream,
    So my love strains to stop
    His pain from overtaking him.

Early life

Jennifer was born into a destitute family as the youngest of 13 children. Their rural house had no running water or indoor plumbing, and only wood heat and single-pane windows to protect them from the long Ontario winters. Although the family's circumstances in relation to others made impressions on her, so did the region's distinct seasons and landscapes. At the same time, despite their disadvantages, reading and the arts were encouraged, and parents and siblings alike enjoyed different forms of writing. At age 9, Jennifer moved to the beautiful coast of British Columbia with her mother and 3 siblings. She focused on poetry from age 11, around the time she started late French Immersion.

Influences

Jennifer excelled in her high school language and literature classes, and especially in poetry. She was further exposed to other cultures and languages through the diversity of the coast area. After a college course, she started working as a legal secretary. There was a bookstore next to her office, and in it she discovered Eastern poetry like Bengal's Rabindranath Tagore, China's Li Po and Du Fu and Japanese haiku. Her modest gleanings from their superlative examples are seen in her use of shorter lines that are simply worded or densely packed, with crisp metaphors and seasonal references.

During that period Jennifer also explored Biblical poetry and its unique aspects, like vivid verbs, concrete words for abstract concepts, short conjunctions for flow, and 'rhymes' of thought – parallel ideas or words used purposefully to connect different lines and allow groupings to make multiple points, and she passed many nights listening to recordings of the psalms.

She later visited West Africa. She spent years managing a modern Guinean music group based in Vancouver and writing its promotional material.

Jennifer's first submission to a poetry magazine in 2007 was accepted, and she now focuses on learning and improving her writing.

About the Author

Jennifer Yeates Camara enjoys different forms of poetry, but the style mostly seen in this collection is architectural.

Lines are built only long enough to hold what is needed. Intimate feelings and rich visuals are described in everyday language that is clear and calm. The minimal verse at times is broken where the lines stand alone or the words at those points become different phrases with those before or after.

Many poems use parallels, or rhymes of thought, to keep ideas finely connected. Yet routinely, they take the reader to unexpected endings. Most are short shots – they may be quickly swallowed but keenly felt.

Jennifer lives with her son Mohamed in Vancouver, Canada. She works as a paralegal in succession planning, supporting the drafting of legal documents.

More of Jennifer's works and background can be found at yeatescamara.com.